Bygone Boston

A Postcard Tour of Beantown

• BY EARL BRECHLIN WITH JOHN BISHOP •

DOWN EAST BOOKS • CAMDEN, MAINE

To my dear, dear Roxie.
You are a delight.
— E.B. —

COPYRIGHT © 2003 BY EARL D. BRECHLIN. ALL RIGHTS RESERVED.
LIBRARY OF CONGRESS CONTROL NUMBER: 2002113591
ISBN 0-89272-569-9
COVER AND BOOK DESIGN BY LURELLE CHEVERIE
RPS · PRINTED IN CHINA
2   4   6   8   9   7   5   3   1
DOWN EAST BOOKS
P.O. BOX 679, CAMDEN ME 04843
BOOK ORDERS: 1-800-766-1670
WWW.DOWNEASTBOOKS.COM

Preface More than a hundred years ago, long before people began lugging early Kodak Brownie cameras around, postcards were a favorite way to document trips and adventures. People collected as well as sent postcards to be able to share with others the wonders and sights they had seen. The bright colors, some even tinted by hand, allowed people to relive their trip and to bring their friends and families along, over and over.

The popularity of postcards exploded, with numerous merchants and photographers competing to offer the widest selection and the most interesting views. Initially, many of the cards were produced in Germany. Later, printers in the United States got in on the craze. Most of the cards in this book come from the peak postcard period, between 1905 and 1920.

Early postcard makers saw their products as interpretations of a scene rather than a strict, literal, photographic portrayals. Many postcards were hand colored, making each one, in effect, an individual work of art. Manufacturers, many of them located far overseas, did not hesitate to alter the original simple black-and-white images, changing colors at will, no matter what instructions may have come from the photographer.

In that era, Boston, without question the "Hub" of New England—if not, as many in Beantown like to think, the universe—was one of the most popular travel destinations. Even today, there are few other cities in this country that can boast as many "firsts," or that hold such a long and marvelous history. Postcards from Boston were mailed to nearly every corner of the country.

While assembling the images for this book, I took a couple of days and prowled the antiques shops of Charles Street and over the river in Cambridge, looking to round out my collection. Pickings were surprisingly slim. It dawned on me later that the place to look for Boston cards was well away from the city, in the villages where the cards were sent to—not where they came from—places where a message from a friend or family member in a faraway place was a treasured keepsake. Following that logic, I found the vast majority of the cards in Maine and Connecticut.

For the people of today, collecting antique postcards—whether from Boston or anywhere else—is a comparatively inexpensive way to hold on to a piece of the past. The affection they engender creates a connection to the past in much the same way that the beauty and history of these special places continue to occupy our hearts. The images in this book, while never intended to be a comprehensive scholarly collection, do provide a wonderful taste—a visual sampling, if you will—of the way things were in Boston more than a hundred years ago. In that respect, they allow people of this century to take a trip not only to a place they know and love well, or may one day hope to visit, but also to a place where no one can ever hope to travel—back to another time. ✍

1. OLIVER WENDELL HOLMES CALLED BOSTON "THE HUB OF THE UNIVERSE," AND EVEN TODAY BOSTONIANS TEND TO AGREE. FROM THE BASIC WHEEL SHAPE OF THE CITY STREETS, TO THE SPOKED B REPRESENTING THE HUB ON THE BOSTON BRUINS' HOCKEY JERSEYS, TO BOSTON'S CULTURAL REPUTATION AS "THE ATHENS OF AMERICA," BOSTONIANS HAVE ALWAYS FELT THAT THEY HOLD A SPECIAL PLACE IN THE GRAND SCHEME OF THINGS. THE SITES ON THIS CARD ARE STILL STANDING. ALL ARE ON THE ROUTE OF BOSTON'S FAMOUS HISTORY WALK, THE FREEDOM TRAIL.

913:—"The Hub," Boston, Mass.

THE HUB

STATE HOUSE.

FANEUIL HALL

KING'S CHAPEL

OLD STATE HOUSE

OLD NORTH CHURCH

BUNKER HILL MONUMENT

2. DESIGNED BY ARCHITECT ALEXANDER PARRIS, AND DEVELOPED AS AN EXTENSION TO THE EXISTING MARKETPLACE AT CHARLES BULFINCH'S FANEUIL HALL, QUINCY MARKET IS BOSTON'S MOST FAMOUS MARKETPLACE. THE CORNERSTONE WAS LAID ON APRIL 27, 1825, AND THE NEW STRUCTURE WAS NAMED IN HONOR OF JOSIAH QUINCY, BOSTON'S SECOND MAYOR (1823–28).

THE PLAN BY ARCHITECTS BENJAMIN AND JANE THOMPSON TO CREATE A "MODERN URBAN MARKET" SAVED QUINCY MARKET FROM URBAN RENEWAL IN 1976. TODAY'S TOURIST DESTINATION AND DOWNTOWN HOT SPOT BEARS LITTLE RESEMBLANCE TO THE BUSTLING SCENE PICTURED HERE; INSTEAD OF PRODUCE, CONTEMPORARY VISITORS TO QUINCY MARKET PURCHASE MERCHANDISE AND FOOD FROM A PLETHORA OF SHOPS AND RESTAURANTS.

Boston Market, Boston, Mass.

AGRICULTURAL WAREHOHSE. AMES PLOW COMPAN

3. Horse-drawn carriages and pedestrians travel down Tremont Street in a scene vaguely reminiscent of today's activity. This view shows Park Street Church on "Brimstone Corner" in the background, with St. Paul's Episcopal Cathedral partially visible on the right. The entrance to Park Street T Station is on the left.

The Park Street Church sits on the site of the 1738 Granary, a long wooden structure designed to hold 12,000 bushels of grain in case of famine. The church was designed by Peter Banner in 1810. William Lloyd Garrison, a prominent Boston abolitionist, gave his first antislavery speech here. His vigorous rhetoric only added to the lore of Brimstone Corner, so called for the fiery religious speakers who expounded there and for the fact that gunpowder was stored in the church basement during the War of 1812.

4. THE FEDERAL BUILDING WAS A "LUCKY" EDIFICE. BOSTON'S
GREAT FIRE OF 1872 OCCURRED EARLY DURING ITS CONSTRUCTION,
THUS HARDLY AFFECTING THE STRUCTURE. DESIGNED IN THE FRENCH
SECOND EMPIRE STYLE, THE POST OFFICE ONCE STOOD BETWEEN
MILK STREET AND WATER STREET. THE GUIDE FOR THE STRANGER IN
BOSTON, PUBLISHED IN 1876, REPORTS ON A TRUE POSTAL BARGAIN:
"THE INLAND POSTAGE (WHICH MUST BE PREPAID) IS 3 CENTS; DOUBLE
LETTERS, TWICE, AND TREBLE LETTERS, TREBLE THOSE RATES."

I don't think you will ever reach this old
inside home. Your postal are fine -
do you know me? Washington tour begun? H.H.A.

5. Not to be confused with Tudor Wharf, and having nothing to do with the Boston Tea Party, "T" Wharf at one time was formally known as Minott's Wharf. It is a piece of an antique structure called the Barricado that once enclosed the Town Cove shipping area and was part of a line of defense that ran from the foot of Copp's Hill to Fort Hill. Boston's waterfront has suffered from a decline in the shipping industry, but in recent times, wealthy Bostonians have called many of the city's oldest wharves home, creating apartments and condominiums along these manmade extensions of the waterfront.

T Wharf, Boston, Mass.

6. OLD CITY HALL ON SCHOOL STREET WAS DESIGNED BY ARTHUR GILMAN AND BUILT DURING THE CIVIL WAR. THE BUILDING SERVED AS BOSTON'S SEAT OF CITY GOVERNMENT FOR A CENTURY, UNTIL THE GOVERNMENT CENTER PLAN CAME TO FRUITION DURING THE 1960S. THE STATUES FLANKING THE ENTRANCE ARE OF BELOVED BOSTON MAYOR JOSIAH QUINCY (HIDDEN IN THIS VIEW) AND ANOTHER PATRIOTIC SON OF BOSTON, BENJAMIN FRANKLIN. OLD CITY HALL IS AN EXAMPLE OF FRENCH SECOND EMPIRE ARCHITECTURE, EXHIBITING A COPPER-PLATED MANSARD ROOF IN THE STYLE OF THE LOUVRE IN PARIS. MAYOR JOHN F. FITZGERALD WAS PRESIDENT JOHN FITZGERALD KENNEDY'S MATERNAL GRANDFATHER.

Hon. John F. Fitzgerald,
Mayor of Boston.

City Hall and Rear View Kings Chapel,
School Street, Boston, Mass.

7. KING'S CHAPEL, THE FIRST ANGLICAN CHURCH IN THE COLONIES, WAS DESIGNED IN 1749. PETER HARRISON, THE ARCHITECT, RAN OUT OF FUNDING BEFORE THE SPIRE COULD BE CONSTRUCTED, SO THE STRUCTURE WAS CONSIDERED COMPLETE AS OF 1754, AND THE CHURCH RETAINED ITS SHORT, STOUT LOOK IN PERPETUITY. ALTHOUGH IT BEGAN ITS CAREER AS AN ANGLICAN CHURCH, KING'S CHAPEL BECAME THE FIRST AMERICAN UNITARIAN CHURCH IN 1789, WHEN THE NEWLY INDEPENDENT AMERICANS ESCHEWED ALL THINGS BRITISH. THE ADJACENT CEMETERY IS THE OLDEST IN BOSTON AND DATES TO 1630. GOVERNORS JOHN WINTHROP AND WILLIAM SHIRLEY ARE INTERRED HERE.

Houghton & Dutton

Tremont Street, showing King's Chapel, Boston, Mass.

213001 (JV)

8. Once the tallest building in Boston, the Ames Building is an example of masonry bearing-wall construction. It was designed by Shepley, Rutan, and Coolidge in 1889. Its Romanesque Revival facade on Court Street is in stark contrast to the famous mirror-walled John Hancock Tower, now the tallest structure on the Boston skyline. Boston's most important daily newspapers, the *Boston Globe* and the *Boston Herald*, can both trace their roots back to Newspaper Row and the historic area surrounding the Ames Building.

News Paper Row
and
Ames Building
(the tallest in
Boston)

Correspondence   *Address*

9. HORACE GRAY AND CHARLES FRANCIS BERNARD, A UNITARIAN MINISTER, FOUNDED BOSTON'S PUBLIC GARDEN AS A BOTANICAL GARDEN IN 1837. ITS DESIGNER, GEORGE V. MEACHUM, THEN DEVELOPED IT INTO ITS CURRENT CONFIGURATION IN 1859. THE PUBLIC GARDEN WAS ONCE A SALT MARSH, BUT NOW IS HOME TO 125 TYPES OF TREES. THE FIRST-EVER EQUESTRIAN STATUE OF GEORGE WASHINGTON WAS INSTALLED THERE IN 1869, AND PRESIDES OVER THIS TRANQUIL SCENE WITH THE STATE HOUSE DOME LOOMING ATOP BEACON HILL IN THE DISTANCE. TODAY THE PARK REMAINS A TWENTY-FOUR-ACRE OASIS IN A GROWING URBAN LANDSCAPE.

E 6416 BIRDS EYE VIEW OF PUBLIC GARDEN, BOSTON, MASS.

10. THE FIRST UNDERWATER TUNNEL OF ITS TYPE BUILT IN AMERICA, THE EAST BOSTON TUNNEL OPENED IN DECEMBER 1904. WHAT STARTED OUT AS A SHORT STREETCAR LINE TO CONNECT EAST BOSTON AND DOWNTOWN BOSTON LATER BECAME, AFTER CONVERSION TO HEAVY RAIL IN THE 1920S, THE BLUE LINE. MORE TUNNELS UNDER THE HARBOR FOLLOWED, INCLUDING THE SUMNER TUNNEL (1934) AND THE CALLAHAN TUNNEL (1961). THE NEWEST UNDERGROUND CONNECTION TO LOGAN AIRPORT, THE TED WILLIAMS TUNNEL, WAS OPENED IN DECEMBER 1995, AS THE FIRST COMPLETED MAJOR COMPONENT OF THE BIG DIG.

Entrance to East Boston Tunnel, E. Boston, Mass.

11. This card depicts a remarkably empty subway scene at the now abandoned Court Street Station. While elevated trains had been in use long before, Boston developed its subway after the state legislature voted, in 1893 and 1894, to authorize its construction. Work began at Boston Public Garden on March 28, 1895, and the line to Park Street Station opened on September 1, 1897. Court Street station was the terminus of the East Boston tunnel from that line's opening until November 1914, when an extension was opened to Bowdoin. To extend the tracks, the floor of Court Street was cut away and a tunnel built below. The stop has been abandoned ever since. When the overhead vent grates are open, the dusty old station can be seen from the platform on the Green Line at Government Center.

E 6403 TUNNEL STATION, COURT ST, BOSTON, MASS.

12. The hustle and bustle on Winter Street in this postcard is familiar to those who know the area today. It is the main walking route between the Park Street T stop and the shopping mecca of Downtown Crossing. Just down the street from where this shot was taken, Edward Filene opened his basement store in 1909. He reportedly sold clothing at such low prices that he failed to make any profit in his first ten years in business. Eventually, he turned the operation around and opened a traditional department store upstairs, which has thrived and become a major chain. Both the basement and main store remain a must-see stop today.

WINTER ST. FROM TREMONT,
BOSTON, MASS.

13. Much of "Old Scollay" has been demolished, leaving the decidedly modern edifices of Government Center and City Hall Plaza. At right, the Sears Crescent, built in 1816, is the lone 21st-century holdover from the pictured scene. An entrance to the Government Center T Station has replaced the kiosk. The square was named for the Scollay Building (demolished prior to this view in 1871), and the building, in turn, derived its name from apothecary William Scollay. During the first half of the twentieth century, until the 1960s, it was considered the "red light district" in Boston.

529. BOSTON, Scollay Square.

14. Named for legendary patriot Samuel Adams, whose statue once stood in the center, Adams Square was another victim of the urban renewal craze of the 1960s. It was located roughly where City Hall and New Congress Street are today, just west of Faneuil Hall. The subway stop at the square was closed in October 1963.

Adams Square, Boston, Mass.

15. A victim of the original Central Artery Project and its elevated highway in the early 1950s, Haymarket Square was a busy commercial center and transportation hub. The Boston City Hospital Relief Station was opened there in 1900 to care for workers injured in industrial accidents. The Haymarket, which during the 1800s was located on Mill Creek, was a prime hub for barge traffic on the Middlesex Canal, which linked the city with farms upstate. Scholars in later years referred to Haymarket as Boston's "gas station," in reference to all the hay that was sold there to "fuel" the horses that pulled Boston's wagons and carriages.

Haymarket Square, Boston, Mass.

16. BOSTON'S FIRE DEPARTMENT HAS THE DISTINCTION OF BEING THE OLDEST PROFESSIONAL DEPARTMENT IN THE NATION, ORGANIZED IN 1678. THE CITY'S FIRST FIRE PREVENTION LAW WAS PASSED IN 1631, PROHIBITING THATCHED ROOFS AND WOODEN CHIMNEYS. SLATE OR "TYLE" ROOFS AND BRICK WALLS WERE REQUIRED IN 1678. STEAM POWER REPLACED HAND-OPERATED PUMPS IN 1859. THE LAST OF BOSTON'S FIRE-HORSE TEAMS, WHICH PULLED STEAM ENGINES ON WAGONS LIKE THE ONE PICTURED, WAS NOT REPLACED UNTIL 1925. DURING THE GREAT FIRE OF BOSTON IN 1872, THIRTEEN PEOPLE WERE KILLED AND 776 BUILDINGS DESTROYED. THE LOSSES WERE ESTIMATED AT MORE THAN $75 MILLION.

Going to the Fire.

17. JUST DOWN FROM THE OLD
STATE HOUSE AT THE CORNER OF
DEVONSHIRE AND STATE STREETS,
A CIRCLE OF COBBLESTONES MARKS
THE SITE OF THE INFAMOUS BOSTON
MASSACRE. ON MARCH 5, 1770,
A SQUAD OF BRITISH TROOPS—TIRED
OF BEING PELTED WITH INSULTS AND
SNOWBALLS, AND EVENTUALLY ROCKS
AND BOTTLES—FIRED ON AN ANGRY
MOB, KILLING FIVE BOSTONIANS. THE
FIRST TO DIE WAS CRISPUS ATTUCKS,
A FREE BLACK MAN. IRONICALLY, THE
SOLDIERS WERE DEFENDED IN COURT
BY JOHN ADAMS AND JOSIAH QUINCY.
THEY WON ACQUITTAL FOR ALL BUT
TWO OF THE TWELVE BRITS ARRESTED
IN THE INCIDENT. THE SONS OF LIB-
ERTY LATER USED SENSATIONALIZED
ACCOUNTS OF THE MASSACRE TO
INFLAME REVOLUTIONARY PASSIONS.

The Spot where the Boston Massacre took Place, March 5, 1770, corner Devonshire and State Street, Boston, Mass.

18. LONG A VITAL LINK BETWEEN SOUTH STATION AND THE OLD COLONY LINES, THE NEW HAVEN RAILROAD, AND THE DOVER STREET COACH YARDS, THESE THREE ROLLING LIFT BRIDGES OVER THE FORT POINT CHANNEL WERE BUILT IN THE LATE 1890S. (THEY HAVE SINCE BEEN DEMOLISHED AS PART OF THE BIG DIG.) PIONEERED IN CHICAGO IN THE EARLY1890S, THE ROLLING LIFT BRIDGE DESIGN SPORTED LARGE CURVED STEEL BEAMS SHAPED LIKE ROCKING CHAIR ROCKERS. WHEN THE BRIDGES WERE RAISED FOR A SHIP TO PASS, THEY WOULD ROLL ALONG THE UNDERLYING STEEL BEAM, WITH GEAR-LIKE TEETH AND POCKETS KEEPING THEM ALIGNED. CONCRETE COUNTER-WEIGHTS ON THE BACK HELPED THEM OPEN WITH MINIMAL EFFORT.

Three Tower Bridges, Boston, Mass.

19. Boston's original Customs House, opened in 1847, was a grand public building, with each Doric column carved from individual pieces of Quincy granite weighing 46 tons. The 30-story tower, designed by Robert S. Peabody and John G. Stearns, was added in 1915. The town's first skyscraper at 498 feet, it remained New England's tallest building until 1965. Since 1985 peregrine falcons have successfully nested on the tower. Unoccupied for more than a dozen years, the structure was converted to vacation timeshares in the late 1990s. An observation deck, museum, and other spaces remain open to the public.

10:—CUSTOM HOUSE TOWER, BOSTON, MASS.

20. AS MOST STUDENTS OF AMERICAN HISTORY KNOW, THE BATTLE OF BUNKER HILL WAS ACTUALLY FOUGHT ON BREED'S HILL ON JUNE 17, 1775. THIS FIRST MAJOR BATTLE OF THE REVOLUTIONARY WAR IS REMEMBERED FOR THE WORDS OF REBEL COLONEL WILLIAM PRESCOTT, WHO TOLD HIS MEN, "DON'T SHOOT UNTIL YOU SEE THE WHITES OF THEIR EYES." THE GRANITE TOWER MONUMENT IS 221 FEET HIGH, WITH 294 STEPS TO GET TO THE TOP. THE CORNERSTONE WAS SET BY THE MARQUIS DE LAFAYETTE ON JULY 17, 1825. THE LAST STONE WAS SET IN JULY 1842. A MAJOR DEDICATION CEREMONY ON JUNE 17, 1843, INCLUDED A SPEECH BY ORATOR DANIEL WEBSTER.

900:—Bunker Hill Monument, Boston, Mass.

21. BORN ON A FARM IN NEW HAMPSHIRE, MARY BAKER EDDY (1821–1910) FOUNDED THE CHURCH OF CHRIST, SCIENTIST, IN 1879. BOSTON'S FIRST CHRISTIAN SCIENCE CHURCH BUILDING, KNOWN AS THE MOTHER CHURCH, WAS BUILT IN 1894 BETWEEN THE SOUTH END AND BACK BAY AREAS. ALTHOUGH IT COULD HOLD A THOUSAND PEOPLE, IT WAS QUICKLY OUTGROWN. THE CORNERSTONE FOR THE MASSIVE DOME THAT DOMINATES THE SITE TODAY WAS LAID IN JULY 1904. NOTED BOSTON ARCHITECT CHARLES BRIGHAM DESIGNED THE STRUCTURE, WHICH CAN SEAT THREE THOUSAND PEOPLE. E. NOYES WHITCOMB WAS THE BUILDER. MOST IN THE CHURCH REFERRED TO THE NEW BUILDING (SHOWN ON LEFT) SIMPLY AS "THE EXTENSION," EVEN THOUGH ITS 224-FOOT HEIGHT DWARFED THE ORIGINAL MOTHER CHURCH.

Christian Science Church, Boston, Mass.

22. One of the more remarkable accomplishments of the Church of Christ, Scientist, is that when its two million-dollar "extension" was dedicated in June 1906, it was debt-free. It features an Aeolian-Skinner Company of Boston organ that boasts more than 13,000 pipes. Newspapers at the time reported that more than 40,000 of the faithful attended the dedication. This card shows the extension being built. A monumental portico, with columns soaring two stories high, was added in 1975.

The 14-acre plaza site now is home not only to the church but also to a recently built 28-story church administration building, a Sunday school building, and the offices of Monitor Radio and the *Christian Science Monitor*, one of the world's most respected newspapers.

CHRISTIAN SCIENCE CHURCH

BOSTON, MASS.

971

23. BUILT ON AN OLD TOWN BURYING GROUND (PRESENTLY THE CORNER OF TREMONT AND SCHOOL STREETS) IN 1688, THE ORIGINAL KING'S CHAPEL WAS TOO SMALL FOR ITS CONGREGATION BY 1749. ARCHITECT PETER HARRISON WAS HIRED TO REPLACE THE ORIGINAL WOODEN BUILDING WITH A NEW EPISCOPAL CHURCH TO RIVAL ANY IN ENGLAND. THE PRESENT STRUCTURE WAS COMPLETED IN 1754. IT WAS THE SEAT OF POWER OF THE ANGLICAN CHURCH IN THE COLONIES UNTIL AFTER THE REVOLUTION, WHEN IT BECAME THE FIRST UNITARIAN CHURCH IN THE NEW NATION.

THE GRAVEYARD NEXT DOOR WAS NOT ASSOCIATED WITH THE CHURCH. IT IS THE FINAL RESTING PLACE OF ELIZABETH PAIN, SAID TO BE THE INSPIRATION FOR NATHANIEL HAWTHORNE'S HESTER PRYNNE IN *THE SCARLET LETTER*.

908 Kings Chapel, Boston, Mass.

24. Irish immigrant Patrick Charles Keely designed Boston's Holy Cross Cathedral, the largest Catholic church in New England, which was dedicated in December 1875. The church's pews can accommodate some two thousand worshipers at once. The roofline of the neo-Gothic church soars 120 feet above the ground on Washington Street in the South End.

William Cardinal O'Connell became archbishop of Boston in 1907 and cardinal in 1911. He performed the wedding of Joseph P. Kennedy and Rose Fitzgerald in October of 1914. Before coming to Boston, he served as bishop of Portland, Maine. Cardinal O'Connell died in 1944. He was followed by Richard Cardinal Cushing.

HIS EMINENCE, CARDINAL O'CONNELL

HOLY CROSS CATHEDRAL, BOSTON, MASS.

25. THE TREMONT TEMPLE, WHICH STILL STANDS TODAY AT 76 TREMONT STREET, WAS DESIGNED BY CLARENCE H. BLACKALL IN 1896. IN ITS DAY IT WAS A FAMOUS BOSTON THEATER, STAGE TO MANY FAMOUS PERFORMERS. CHARLOTTE CUSHMAN, FANNY KEMBLE, AND DANIEL WEBSTER, ALONG WITH EDWARD EVERETT AND JENNY LIND, HAVE GRACED THE BUILDING, NOW HOUSING OFFICES AND A CHURCH. NEARBY, BOSTON'S PRESENT-DAY THEATER DISTRICT CARRIES ON THE TRADITION OF THE TREMONT TEMPLE.

MESSAGE MAY BE WRITTEN ON THIS SIDE ADDRESS TO BE WRITTEN ON THIS SIDE

POST CARD

QUALITY

TREMONT TEMPLE, BOSTON, MASS.

37003

26. A KEY PART OF THE CHAIN OF BOSTON'S "EMERALD NECKLACE"— A STRING OF PARKS DESIGNED BY NOTED LANDSCAPE ARCHITECT FREDERICK LAW OLMSTED—THE CHARLES STREET ESPLANADE RAN FROM CAMBRIDGE STREET TO BEACON STREET ESPLANADE. THE RIVER AT THIS POINT IS DAMMED, MAKING IT A FAVORITE PLACE FOR SAILING AND BOAT RACES. ELSEWHERE ALONG THE ESPLANADE, A FAVORITE HAUNT OF BICYCLISTS AND JOGGERS, IS THE SUMMER HOME OF THE BOSTON POPS ORCHESTRA, WHICH PERFORMS REGULARLY AT THE HATCH SHELL.

79:—Charles St. Esplanade, Boston, Mass.

31057

27. A FAVORITE SEASIDE ESCAPE IN THE TOWN'S EARLY DAYS, SOUTH BOSTON'S CITY POINT OFFERED TIDAL OCEAN SWIMMING AND BOATING IN THE SHELTERED WATERS OF "THE BOWL." THE IMPOSING STRUCTURE ON THE LANDWARD END OF THE CAUSEWAY IS THE HEAD HOUSE BATHHOUSE FOR MARINE PARK, WHICH WAS THE SEASIDE TERMINUS FOR FREDERICK LAW OLMSTED'S EMERALD NECKLACE OF PARKS AROUND BOSTON.

FORT INDEPENDENCE, A LOW, PENTAGONAL GRANITE STRUCTURE ON CASTLE ISLAND, CAN BE SEEN IN THE BACKGROUND. IT WAS BUILT IN THE MID-1800S AND IS THE LAST OF EIGHT MILITARY INSTALLATIONS BUILT AROUND BOSTON HARBOR. THE ISLAND IS CONSIDERED THE OLDEST CONTINUALLY FORTIFIED SITE IN BRITISH NORTH AMERICA.

FROM THE
McPHAIL PIANO CO.
BOSTON

Boston, Mass. City Point.

28. THE TRADITION OF THE SOUTH BOSTON YACHT CLUB GOES BACK AS FAR AS FEBRUARY 1868, WHEN THEIR FIRST MEETING TOOK PLACE IN A BOATHOUSE BELONGING TO ARTHUR SCOTT. IN APRIL 1877, THE YACHT CLUB WAS INCORPORATED UNDER THE LAWS OF THE COMMONWEALTH OF MASSACHUSETTS "FOR THE PURPOSE OF ENCOURAGING YACHT BUILDING AND NATURAL SCIENCE." THE CLUB BUILT ITS FIRST BUILDING IN 1868, THEN MOVED THE STRUCTURE TO A NEW LOCATION LESS THAN THREE YEARS LATER. A GREATLY ENLARGED AND REMODELED CLUBHOUSE WAS DEDICATED AT THEIR STRANDWAY SITE (NOW CALLED DAY BLVD.) IN 1886, ONLY TO BE DEMOLISHED AND REPLACED BY THEIR CURRENT BUILDING (SHOWN HERE) IN 1899.

South Boston Yacht Club.   Boston, Mass.

29. Anchored in Dorchester Bay in Boston Harbor near City Point, this floating lifesaving station was built in 1896. (A report the previous year referred to "numerous fatal accidents that have occurred in the waters of Dorchester Bay.") Crews stood by with pulling boats to render assistance to people on yachts and sailboats that encountered trouble. One of the first stations in the country established primarily to assist recreational boaters, it was rebuilt in 1913, only to be discontinued in 1930.

CITY POINT LIFE SAVING STATION, BOSTON HARBOR, MASS.

30. REVERE BEACH IS A CONTRADICTION. ITS ACCESSIBILITY BY PUBLIC TRANSPORT AND THE FACT THAT IT IS ONE OF THE CLOSEST PUBLIC BEACHES TO DOWNTOWN BOSTON SHOULD MAKE IT ONE OF THE MOST DESIRABLE SPOTS IN ALL OF MASSACHUSETTS. ON THE FLIP SIDE, ITS PROXIMITY TO THE CITY ALSO MAKES IT ONE OF THE MOST OVERUSED BEACHES DURING THE SUMMER. THAT, PLUS POLLUTION PROBLEMS AND THE EVER-PRESENT LOGAN AIRPORT FLIGHT PATTERN, MAKE BEACH-GOING IN THE TWENTY-FIRST CENTURY A MIXED BAG AT BEST. BUT TO THE PEOPLE PICTURED HERE, REVERE BEACH CA. 1900 WAS A PARADISE, THANKS TO ITS LOCATION AND TO THE POPULAR AMUSEMENT PARK ALONG ITS BOARDWALK.

Revere Beach. *Please settle that bill will see you Sunday night*

31. Like so many other points of interest in Boston, Boston Harbor Light was the "first of its kind" in North America. A bill to build the lighthouse was passed in July 1715. A stone tower was built on Little Brewster Island, and the beacon was lit for the first time on September 14, 1716. A tax of a penny per ton on all cargo transiting the harbor paid for its construction. A cannon served for the fog signal. During the Revolution, the lighthouse was burned or destroyed and then repaired several times. It was rebuilt to a height of 75 feet in 1783, and raised to the existing height of 89 feet (shown here) in 1859. The second-order Fresnel lens installed at that time is still in use today. On April 16, 1998, Boston Harbor Light was the last in the nation to be automated.

BOSTON LIGHT, MASS

32. Bug Light was built in 1856 at the end of the Spit, a sandbar near the entrance to a major shipping channel. It earned its name from its unique spindly appearance. A red lamp on the roof of the three-story structure helped mariners avoid Harding's Ledge, several miles away. One of Bug Light's earliest keepers was James Turner, reputed to be a pirate with blood on his hands. There were even reports of buried treasure nearby. The stone bulkheads were built to prevent ice from damaging the tower's metal legs. Flames from a blowtorch used for maintenance reportedly sparked the fire that destroyed the structure on June 7, 1929. A small automated light on a metal tower marks the spot today.

2868 — Bug Light, Boston Harbor, Mass.

33. LOCATED ON BOSTON HARBOR'S LONGEST ISLAND, LONG ISLAND LIGHT HAS SOMETIMES BEEN CALLED THE INNER HARBOR LIGHT. FOUR DIFFERENT TOWERS HAVE STOOD ATOP THE HEADLAND, THE FIRST MADE OF GRANITE AND LOOSE STONE CONSTRUCTED IN 1819, THE SECOND AND THIRD OF IRON, AND THE FOURTH (PICTURED) BUILT OF BRICK IN 1901. WHEN THE FIRST CAST-IRON TOWER WAS ERECTED IN 1844, IT WAS THE FIRST OF ITS TYPE IN THE NATION. A SECOND CAST-IRON TOWER FOLLOWED IN 1881. LONG ISLAND LIGHT WAS AUTOMATED IN 1929. IT WAS DISCONTIN-UED IN 1982, BUT REACTIVATED THREE YEARS LATER WHEN A SOLAR-POWERED BEACON WAS INSTALLED. A BRIDGE CONNECTING LONG ISLAND WITH QUINCY WAS BUILT IN 1951. THE KEEPER'S HOUSE AND RELATED BUILDINGS NO LONGER STAND.

Long Island Light, Boston Harbor.

34. GRAVES LIGHT SITS ON BARREN LEDGES NAMED IN THE 1600s FOR VICE ADMIRAL THOMAS GRAVES. THE 113-FOOT GRANITE TOWER WAS BUILT IN 1905 FROM STONE QUARRIED AT ROCKPORT ON CAPE ANN. THE TOWER'S FOUNDATION SITS JUST FOUR FEET ABOVE THE LOW TIDE MARK. WHEN LIT FOR THE FIRST TIME ON SEPTEMBER 1, 1905, THE BEACON WAS SAID TO BE THE MOST POWERFUL IN NEW ENGLAND. THE MASSIVE FIRST-ORDER FRESNEL LENS, MORE THAN TWELVE FEET HIGH, FLOATED ON HUNDREDS OF POUNDS OF MERCURY.

EARLY KEEPERS SOMETIMES CAUGHT THEIR OWN LOBSTERS IN NEAR-BY WATERS. IN 1947, PRODUCER DAVID O. SELZNICK FILMED PART OF THE MOVIE *PORTRAIT OF JENNIE* AT GRAVES LIGHT. IN OCTOBER 1991, THE FIERCE TEMPEST MADE FAMOUS IN *THE PERFECT STORM* SWEPT AWAY THE FOG SIGNAL HOUSE AND CAUSED OTHER MAJOR DAMAGE.

The Graves Light, Boston Harbor.

35. WITH A STURDY IRON HULL, LIGHTSHIP *LV 54* STOOD GUARD OFF THE COAST OF BOSTON FROM 1894 UNTIL 1940. BUILT IN 1892 FOR THE THEN PRINCELY SUM OF $70,000, THE STEAM-POWERED VESSEL BOASTED TWO LANTERNS CONTAINING EIGHT LAMPS AND REFLECTORS EACH. WHILE IN SERVICE, SHE WAS BUMPED AND SCRAPED BY NUMEROUS VESSELS WITH LITTLE SERIOUS EFFECT UNTIL, ON DECEMBER 20,1935, SHE WAS STRUCK HARD BY THE BRITISH STEAMER *SEVEN SEAS SPRAY*. THE LIGHTSHIP'S CREW MANAGED TO STEM THE INRUSHING SEA WATER BY STUFFING SACKS OF COAL INTO THE GASH IN THE HULL. AT VARIOUS TIMES DURING HER SERVICE, *LV 54* ALSO SPENT TIME AS A PILOT VESSEL GUIDING MARINERS OFF NANTUCKET. SHE WAS DECOMMISSIONED IN 1946.

BOSTON LIGHT SHIP, BOSTON HARBOR, MASS. *are pretty. G. R. Beal. 9-12-'07 Many thanks for your postals. They*

36. Opened on January 1, 1899, South Station epitomized the transportation hustle and bustle of the dawning new century. The elevated tracks over Dewey Square, in the foreground, were removed just before World War II. South Station was served by the New York, New Haven, and Hartford Railroad as well as the Boston and Albany Railroad. It replaced several small stations that had served those lines and others, including the Old Colony and Boston and Providence Railroads. In 1965 the Massachusetts Bay Transportation Authority (MBTA) began subsidizing commuter rail transport on lines servicing both North and South Stations. It now runs both stations, four subway lines, buses, and ferries.

BOSTON, MASS. SOUTH TERMINAL STATION

37. Locomotives belching steam and smoke are ready to depart from the train shed at South Station. Designed by the Boston firm of Shepley, Rutan, and Coolidge, the $3.6 million South Terminal Station was reported to be the busiest in the country until Grand Central in New York surpassed it in the 1930s. It sported a massive steel and glass train shed over the tracks. Due to corrosion aggravated by salt air from the nearby harbor, the train shed was torn down in the early 1930s. As part of the Central Artery Project, South Station underwent a major renovation beginning in the 1990s. The bus station is also now part of the complex. It sits astride the passenger rail tracks.

BOSTON, MASS., TRAIN SHED, SOUTH TERMINAL STATION.

38. THE FIRST NORTH STATION (SHOWN HERE) WAS BUILT TO HANDLE BOSTON AND MAINE, MAINE CENTRAL, AND CANADIAN PACIFIC RAILROAD TRAINS ENTERING THE CITY IN THE LATE 1890S. IT WAS REPLACED BY A SECOND STATION IN 1927, WHICH INCLUDED THE 18,500-SEAT BOSTON GARDEN ABOVE THE STATION FACILITY. THE PRESIDENT OF MADISON SQUARE GARDEN, TEX RICKARD, HAD BUILT BOSTON GARDEN FIRST, CALLING IT BOSTON MADISON SQUARE GARDEN, THOUGH NOT LONG AFTER ITS OPENING IN 1928 THE MADISON SQUARE REFERENCE WAS DROPPED. "THE GARDEN" WAS TORN DOWN IN NOVEMBER 1997.

925:—North Station, Boston, Mass.

39. WHEN IT OPENED IN 1901, THE SULLIVAN SQUARE STATION,
IN CHARLESTOWN, WAS THE LARGEST TRANSIT FACILITY IN ALL
OF NORTH AMERICA. THE COMPLEX INCLUDED TRACKS FOR
MAINLINE TRAINS, ELEVATED CARS, AND TROLLEYS, AS WELL AS
YARDS AND A REPAIR SHOP. IN LATER YEARS, BUS FACILITIES
WERE ADDED. TWO MAJOR FIRES TOOK THEIR TOLL ON THE HIGH,
VAULTED STEEL AND GLASS STRUCTURE IN THE 1960S, AND
THE STATION CLOSED IN 1975.

THE STATION PLATFORM SHOWN HERE SPORTS A SIGN THAT
MANY T RIDERS TODAY WOULD AGREE WITH: "RUNNING AGAINST
OTHERS, PUSHING, AND OTHER DISORDERLY CONDUCT IS PROHIB-
ITED. PASSENGERS MUST CONDUCT THEMSELVES WITH DUE
REGARD TO THE RIGHTS AND SAFETY OF OTHERS."

NOTICE

RUNNING AGAINST OTHERS, PUSHING
OTHER DISORDERLY CONDUCT
PROHIBITED. PASSENGERS MUST
CONDUCT THEMSELVES WITH REGARD
FOR THE SAFETY OF OTHERS

HIGHLAND AVE
SOMERVILLE

531. SULLIVAN SQUARE ELEVATED STATION, CHARLESTOWN, MASS.

40. Built in 1723, the Episcopal Old North Church, Boston's oldest, is one of the best-known American landmarks. It entered the history books on the evening of April 18, 1775, when two lanterns were lit in the 191-foot steeple at the request of Paul Revere. The purpose: to warn patriots on the Charlestown shore that the Redcoats were crossing the Charles River on their way to Concord, Lexington, and a rendezvous with the "shot heard round the world." A plaque in a courtyard at the church reads "Eternal vigilance is the price of liberty." Few remember the name of the man who lit the lanterns—church sexton Robert Newman.

13:—CHRIST CHURCH (OLD NORTH), BOSTON, MASS.

41. One of Boston's oldest buildings, the Old South Church traces its origins to 1669, when dissenting parishioners broke from the First Church of Boston to establish the Third Church, later known as Old South Church. The first meeting-house on the site was built in 1670. The existing structure, pictured here before the turn of the century, was built in 1729 at the corner of Washington and Milk Streets.

Benjamin Franklin was baptized in the church in 1706. In 1773 Samuel Adams made his call for the Boston Tea Party here. Now used as an arts center and history museum, the church counted Phillis Wheatley, the first published African-American poetess, among its members. Old South Church became the first building in the country to be pre-served because of its architectural and historic significance.

THIS SPACE FOR WRITING

OLD SOUTH CHURCH, BOSTON, MASS.

42. NOW CALLED THE LONGFELLOW BRIDGE, THIS SPAN
HAS APPEARED IN MORE MOVIES AND TELEVISION SHOWS
THAN MOST OF BOSTON'S PROFESSIONAL THESPIANS.
FEATURED PROMINENTLY IN THE OPENING SEQUENCE OF
SPENSER FOR HIRE AND SCENES FROM *GOOD WILL HUNTING*,
THIS HANDSOME TURRETED BRIDGE MAKES FOR A HAPPY
TRANSITION BETWEEN BEACON HILL AND CAMBRIDGE, AND
IS A VERY RECOGNIZABLE LANDMARK ON THE CHARLES RIVER.
ENGINEERS PLANNED FOR THE FUTURE WHEN THE BRIDGE
WAS BUILT, LEAVING SPACE FOR THE T TRACKS THAT NOW
CROSS THE CENTER OF THE SPAN.

New West Boston Bridge, Boston, Mass.

43. Long before Boston was torn apart by the Big Dig, the city was home to the steel cantilevered-truss Mystic River Bridge, which connected the Charlestown section of Boston with Chelsea. It opened to traffic in February 1950. Shown here in a view from the Bunker Hill Monument, the bridge was built for $27 million by the American Bridge Company over the spot where North America's first ferry operated in 1631. The two-mile modern structure was later renamed the Maurice J. Tobin Memorial Bridge in honor of the former mayor, state representative, governor, and labor secretary.

A trip to her grandfather's house along the Mystic River in 1844 inspired Medford abolitionist Lydia Mariah Child to pen the poem "Over the River and Through the Woods."

"THE MYSTIC RIVER BRIDGE" Connecting Boston, Mass. with Northern New England   B-55

"Photo U. S. Steel Corp."

44. THE FENWAY (PART OF OLMSTED'S EMERALD NECKLACE) HAS NOT AGED WELL, AND TODAY'S TOURISTS WILL BE HARD-PRESSED TO FIND THE RUSTIC AGASSIZ BRIDGE IN THE GREEN AREA BETWEEN HUNTINGTON AVENUE AND KENMORE SQUARE. NONETHELESS, THIS FIVE-SPAN BRICK STRUCTURE, BUILT IN 1887, IS STILL THERE AND STILL CARRYING VEHICLES TODAY. DESPITE THE OVERGROWN BRUSH AND CRACKED CONCRETE, THE BRIDGE BEARS AN ILLUSTRIOUS NAME. HARVARD ZOOLOGIST LOUIS AGASSIZ (1807–73) WAS ONE OF WRITER HENRY ADAMS'S FAVORITE PROFESSORS IN COLLEGE AND WAS POPULAR IN TRANSCENDENTALIST CIRCLES.

Agassiz Bridge, Back Bay Fens, Boston, Mass.

212459

45. IN THE YEARS FOLLOWING THE INTRODUCTION OF THE "HORSELESS CARRIAGE" TO BOSTON, JUST ABOUT ANY STREET MUST HAVE SEEMED LIKE A SPEEDWAY, AS THIS DEPICTION OF THE ROAD THROUGH THE BACK BAY FENS SUGGESTS. THE DOME OF THE MOTHER CHURCH OF THE CHRISTIAN SCIENTISTS IS VISIBLE BEYOND.

THE ONE FORM OF RACING THAT STILL TAKES OVER BOSTON STREETS. EACH YEAR IS THE BOSTON MARATHON. THE BOSTON ATHLETIC ASSOCIATION HELD ITS FIRST MARATHON (WITH A LENGTH OF 24.5 MILES) ON APRIL 19, 1897. THERE WERE FIFTEEN STARTERS. JOHN J. MCDERMOT OF NEW YORK WON WITH A TIME OF 2:55:10. THE COURSE WAS LENGTHENED TO A FULL OLYMPIC 26 MILES, 385 YARDS, IN 1927. IN 1996, A RECORD 38,708 RUNNERS STARTED THE RACE.

The Speedway, Back Bay Fens, Boston, Mass.

212458

46. TWO OF THE FENWAY'S MOST IMPORTANT LANDMARKS, ISABELLA STEWART GARDNER'S HOUSE AND SIMMONS COLLEGE, APPEAR ON THIS CARD. WILLARD T. SEARS BEGAN HIS DESIGN FOR THE HOUSE IN 1899, AND THE LANDMARK WAS OPENED IN 1903. TALES ABOUT "MRS. JACK" WALKING A LION OR TAKING UP BUDDHISM PALE IN COMPARISON TO THE HOUSE-MUSEUM THAT REMAINS A TESTAMENT TO HER AMAZING PERSONALITY. HER WILL STIPULATED THAT EACH PIECE OF ART OR FURNITURE IN THE BUILDING MUST REMAIN IN THE EXACT SPOT WHERE SHE PLACED IT. AN EXTRAORDINARILY COMPLEX INTERIOR LIES BEHIND THE SOOTHINGLY SIMPLE FACADE. NEXT DOOR, SIMMONS COLLEGE HAS WELCOMED FEMALE SCHOLARS SINCE JOHN SIMMONS FOUNDED THE SCHOOL IN 1899.

MRS. JACK GARDNERS RESIDENCE AND SIMMONS COLLEGE, BOSTON, MASS.

47. THE THIRD-OLDEST GENERAL HOSPITAL IN THE COUNTRY, MASSACHUSETTS GENERAL WAS FOUNDED IN 1811. IT INCLUDED ONE OF THE FIRST THREE NURSING SCHOOLS IN THE NATION TO BE BASED ON THE PRINCIPLES OF FLORENCE NIGHTINGALE. NOTED BOSTON ARCHITECT CHARLES BULFINCH DESIGNED THE HOSPITAL BUILDING ON FRUIT STREET IN 1817. IT OPENED IN 1823.

ALTHOUGH OTHER PHYSICIANS WERE THE FIRST TO USE ETHER AS A GENERAL ANESTHETIC, DR. WILLIAM T. G. MORTON CON-DUCTED THE FIRST RECORDED SUCCESSFUL DEMONSTRATION OF ITS USE AT MASS GENERAL ON OCTOBER 16, 1846. DR. JOHN COLLINS WARREN, WHO PERFORMED THE SURGERY, IS REPORTED TO HAVE REMARKED, "GENTLEMEN, THIS IS NO HUMBUG."

BULFINCH BUILDING, THE MASSACHUSETTS GENERAL HOSPITAL, BOSTON, MASS.

48. THE STATELY WHITE MARBLE BUILDINGS OF THE MOST FAMOUS MEDICAL COLLEGE IN THE WORLD ARE TUCKED NEATLY ONTO LONGWOOD AVENUE AND AVENUE LOUIS PASTEUR IN THE FENWAY SECTION OF BOSTON — NOT IN CAMBRIDGE WITH THE REST OF HARVARD UNIVERSITY. IN 1907, SHEPLEY, RUTAN, AND COOLIDGE DESIGNED THE HARVARD MEDICAL SCHOOL CAMPUS IN THE CLASSICAL REVIVAL STYLE.

HARVARD MEDICAL SCHOOL, BOSTON MASS.

49. Located between Washington Street and City Hall Avenue, Pie Alley (historians favor Pi as the spelling) was a favorite haunt of job printers, newsboys, and other downtown Boston denizens. A letterpress print job was "pied" when it was dropped or messed up. Printers often represented this term with the Greek character π.

At the left in this image is a Boston police officer, sporting the same kind of hat as an English bobby. The service, the oldest in the country, grew out of a tradition of night watch established in 1635. The City of Boston Police Department was officially established in 1854 and modeled on the police force in London. The first motor patrol, in a chauffeur-driven Stanley Steamer, began in 1903.

GRIDLEY'S

Pie Alley,
Boston, Mass.

50. AHH, FENWAY. IN 1912, RED SOX OWNER JOHN I. TAYLOR BUILT THE GRANDE DAME OF MAJOR LEAGUE BASEBALL BALL YARDS IN THE FENWAY SECTION OF BOSTON AND NAMED IT AFTER THE NEIGHBORHOOD BETWEEN LANDSDOWNE AND JERSEY STREETS. THIS VIEW WAS CAPTURED BEFORE LATER RENOVATIONS, AND SHOWS FENWAY AS A SINGLE-DECK BALLPARK. LEGEND HAS IT THAT MANY OF THE SEATS SHOWN HERE REMAIN IN USE.

UNDER ANOTHER OWNER, THE VENERABLE TOM YAWKEY, THE PARK UNDERWENT A MAJOR RECONSTRUCTION IN 1934, INCLUDING THE ADDITION OF CONCRETE BLEACHERS IN CENTER FIELD AND THE AUGMENTATION OF THE EXISTING GRANDSTANDS FROM LEFT TO RIGHT FIELDS. TODAY, THE BEHEMOTH GLASS-WALLED 600 CLUB SECTION DOMINATES THE AREA BEHIND HOME PLATE.

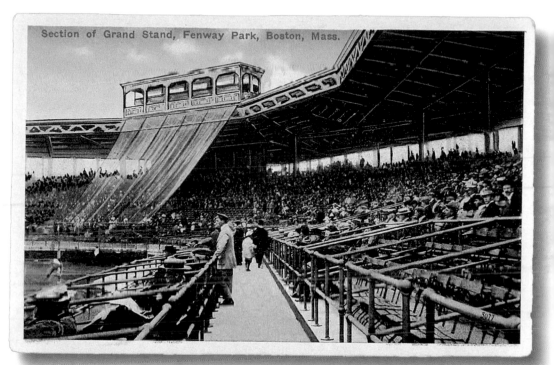

Section of Grand Stand, Fenway Park, Boston, Mass.

51. THE FAMOUS DOME OF THE MASSACHUSETTS INSTITUTE OF TECHNOLOGY LOOMS OVER THE BANKS OF THE CHARLES RIVER IN THIS VIEW OF CAMBRIDGE. WILLIAM WELLS BOSWORTH (AN MIT GRADUATE WHO ALSO DESIGNED THE UNIVERSITY OF MINNESOTA) DESIGNED IT, AND THE REST OF MIT'S MOST RECOGNIZABLE BUILDINGS. THE MACLAURIN AND ROGERS BUILDINGS WERE PROMINENTLY DISPLAYED IN THE ACADEMY AWARD-WINNING MOVIE *GOOD WILL HUNTING*, WRITTEN BY CAMBRIDGE NATIVES BEN AFFLECK AND MATT DAMON.

NOTE THE STREETCAR TRAVELING ACROSS THE HARVARD/ MASSACHUSETTS AVENUE BRIDGE. TODAY, BUSES SERVE THIS ROUTE FROM BOSTON TO CAMBRIDGE.

970 Massachusetts Institute Technology and Harvard Bridge

from Massachusetts Avenue, Boston, Mass.

52. BEGINNING IN EARLY SPRING AND CONTINUING EVEN THROUGH THE FALL, BOSTONIANS HAVE ALWAYS USED THE CHARLES RIVER FOR FUN AND RECREATION. THIS IDYLLIC SCENE—LOCATED FAR INLAND NEAR WHAT IS NOW THE GREEN LINE'S RIVERSIDE T STATION—IS DUPLICATED EACH DAY FROM BASES UP AND DOWN THE CHARLES, ALONG THE ESPLANADE, ACROSS THE RIVER ON MEMORIAL DRIVE IN CAMBRIDGE, AND ALSO ON SOLDIERS FIELD ROAD IN ALLSTON/BRIGHTON. AMATEUR AND COLLEGIATE BOATHOUSES ALSO LINE THE BANKS OF THE RIVER, AND CREWS VIE FOR ROWING SUPERIORITY DURING THE FAMOUS "HEAD OF THE CHARLES" REGATTA, HELD EACH YEAR IN OCTOBER.

U. S. Series 150/4.   Canoeing on Charles River, Boston, Mass.

53. Built by Harvey Parker in 1855 on the corner of School and Tremont Streets, where the Boston Massacre took place, the Parker House bills itself as the oldest continuously operated hotel in North America. From its kitchens came the first Parker House rolls, Boston cream pie, and the term *SCROD*, which means fresh fish of the day. Among those who once walked its halls were General Ulysses S. Grant, Alexander Graham Bell, Henry Wadsworth Longfellow, Ralph Waldo Emerson, Henry David Thoreau, and Charles Dickens. John F. Kennedy announced his bid for Congress in 1953 at the Parker House. Among its employees were two who later found fame: Malcolm X once worked there as a busboy, and Ho Chi Minh, was employed in the kitchen in 1915.

Parker House, Boston, Mass.

54. Built in 1901 at a cost of $100,000, the Hotel Lenox presides over the Boylston Street finish line of the annual BAA Boston Marathon. It took only eight months for the George A. Fuller Company to build the hotel, named for the wife of George III, ruler of Great Britain during the American Revolution. Lucia Boomer, then-owner of the Lenox and the original Waldorf Astoria in New York City, decided on the name to honor the anniversary of more than 150 years of peace between England and North America. The Lenox was renovated in 1997 at a cost of $20 million.

For correspondence only.

HOTEL LENOX

BOYLSTON & EXETER STREET, BOSTON, MASS.

3OO16

LENOX

55. SEAFOOD IS A PASSION FOR BOSTONIANS, AND THAT HAS HELD TRUE SINCE THE CITY'S BEGINNINGS. THE HOTEL PIERONI AND ITS SEA GRILL, WITH ITS BRANCHES IN PARK SQUARE AND ON STUART STREET, TITILLATED THE PALATES OF BOSTONIANS AT THE BEGINNING OF THE TWENTIETH CENTURY. TODAY, SEVERAL BOSTON RESTAURANTS—INCLUDING DURGIN PARK AND THE FAMOUS LEGAL SEAFOODS, WHOSE CLAM CHOWDER IS OF PRESIDENTIAL INAUGURAL FAME—SATISFY APPETITES AND VIE FOR SUPERIORITY IN A VERY DISCRIMINATING MARKET.

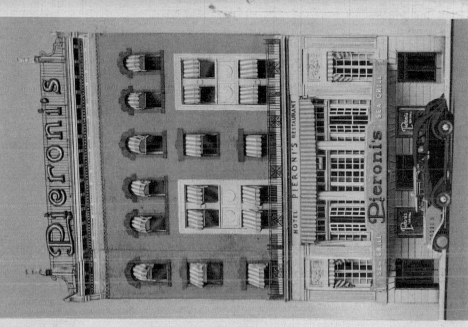

HOTEL PIERONI, 7-8 PARK SQ., BOSTON—FAMOUS FOR TS SEA GRILL

OTHER GRILLS AT 13 STUART ST. AND 601 WASHINGTON ST., BOSTON

56. Constructed on the original site of the Museum of Fine Arts, and now named the Fairmont Copley Plaza, this famous hotel opened in 1912. It was designed by Boston architect Clarence Blackall and Henry Hardenberg, the architect of the Plaza Hotel and the Dakota apartment building in New York City. The hotel has an ongoing artistic tradition and has been featured in several modern motion pictures, including *The Firm* and *Blown Away*. Famed Boston artist John Singer Sargent, who produced several paintings now hanging in the present Museum of Fine Arts on Huntington Avenue, rented a suite of rooms here from 1919 until his death in 1925.

The Copley-Plaza, Boston, Mass.

57. DESIGNED IN 1912, THE TEA COURT OF THE (FAIRMONT)
COPLEY PLAZA HOTEL NO LONGER SERVES HIGH TEA—A TRUE
TRAGEDY, AS THIS WONDERFUL, ELEGANT, HIGH-CEILINGED
ROOM OVERLOOKING COPLEY PLACE HAD BEEN A HIGH-
SOCIETY HAUNT SINCE ITS INCEPTION.

Tea-Room, The Copley-Plaza, Boston, Mass.

58. Called "a city within a city," the Statler Hotel is now known as the Boston Park Plaza. Opened in March 1927, it was created by E. M. Statler, who believed that hotels "should be something of a museum, exposing the traveler, perhaps for the first time, to excellence in art." Along with this artistic function, still embraced today, the Statler was the first hotel to have a radio and cold running water in every room. Today the building is a favorite site for conventions and other functions due to its downtown location and proximity to Boston's theater district.

Statler Hotel, Boston, Mass.

B-22

59. NOW OFFERING LUXURY ACCOMMODATIONS AND OFFICE SPACE, THE BEAUTIFUL HOTEL SOMERSET HAS HARDLY CHANGED SINCE THIS CARD WAS DESIGNED AT THE BEGINNING OF THE TWENTIETH CENTURY. SURELY, THE NEIGHBORHOOD STILL LOOKS SOMEWHAT SIMILAR ON THE COMMONWEALTH AVENUE SIDE, BUT TODAY THE BUILDING IS BORDERED BY THE MASSACHUSETTS TURNPIKE EXTENSION AND A FENWAY OFF-RAMP.

Hotel Somerset, Boston, Mass.

Our figures reported are Mrs. McPherSon - Richer & Hughes.
H. M. B.   2-17-07

60. ANYONE WHO ATTENDED A CONVENTION, CONFERENCE, OR TRADE SHOW IN BOSTON BEFORE THE ADVENT OF HYNES CONVENTION CENTER OR THE BOSTON GARDEN PROBABLY WALKED INTO THIS INTERESTING BUILDING. ALTHOUGH IT WAS BASICALLY JUST A LARGE WAREHOUSE-LIKE STRUCTURE, THE VARIOUS BOAT, DOG, AUTO, AND FLOWER SHOWS THAT GRACED THE FLOOR OF THE MECHANICS BUILDING KEPT HAPPY CROWDS COMING. OPENED IN 1881, THE MECHANICS BUILDING HOSTED AN INAUGURATION CELEBRATION IN 1922 FOR "THE PEOPLE'S MAYOR," JAMES MICHAEL CURLEY, WHICH DREW 12,000 CHEERING PEOPLE. THE BUILDING WAS RAZED IN 1959 TO MAKE WAY FOR THE PRUDENTIAL TOWER PROJECT THAT NOW PROVIDES THE CITY ONE OF ITS MOST RECOGNIZABLE BUILDINGS.

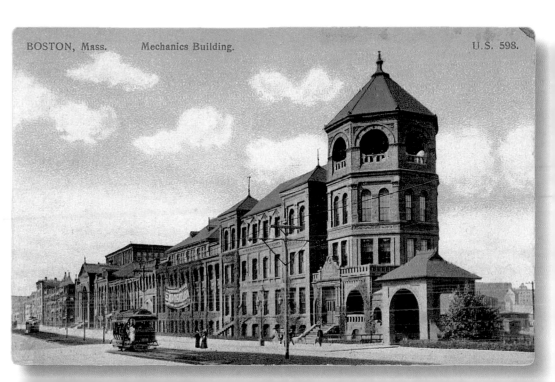

BOSTON, Mass.   Mechanics Building.   U.S. 598.

61. THE CHARLESTOWN NAVY YARD, PICTURED HERE, WAS BUILT IN 1800 ON FORTY-THREE ACRES AT MOULTON'S POINT—THE SAME SPOT WHERE THE BRITISH LANDED TO BEGIN THEIR MARCH TO BREED'S HILL, FOR THE MISNAMED AND PIVOTAL BATTLE OF BUNKER HILL. IN ITS HEYDAY, THE NAVY YARD EMPLOYED 50,000 WORKERS. IN 1943 IT PRODUCED FORTY-SIX DESTROYERS. TODAY, THE NAVY YARD IS HOME TO A VERY FAMOUS WAR OF 1812—ERA VESSEL, THE U.S.S. *CONSTITUTION*, AND THE WORLD WAR II DESTROYER *CASSIN YOUNG*. THIS CARD DEPICTS DRY DOCK #2 WITH THE SHIP *MARYLAND* IN THE FOREGROUND. NOTE THE FIGURES IN WHITE UNIFORMS NEAR THE RUDDER.

Opening of the
Boston Navy Yard,
New Dry Dock,
August 12, 1905.

62. PADDLE-DRIVEN, UNDERGRADUATE-POWERED SWAN BOATS HAVE GRACED THE POND AT THE BOSTON PUBLIC GARDEN SINCE THE PAGET FAMILY STARTED THE TRADITION IN 1877. INSPIRED BY ELEMENTS OF WAGNER'S OPERA *LOHENGRIN*, THE BOATS STILL CARRY UP TO TWENTY PASSENGERS EACH AROUND THE MANMADE LAGOON. THE PUBLIC GARDEN ALSO HAS SPECIAL SIGNIFICANCE IN THE WORLD OF CHILDREN'S LITERATURE AS THE SETTING OF ROBERT MCCLOSKEY'S 1941 CLASSIC, *MAKE WAY FOR DUCKLINGS*. THE SITE OF THE OFT-STOLEN STATUES OF THESE FAMOUS FOWL IS A POPULAR SPOT FOR PHOTOGRAPHS.

SWAN BOAT ON THE LAKE,
PUBLIC GARDEN,
BOSTON, MASS.

63. A POPULAR SKATING SPOT IN WINTER, THE FROG POND HAS REMAINED A MANDATORY STOP FOR STROLLING COUPLES ON SATURDAYS AND SUNDAY, AS WELL AS THE SITE OF LUNCH-HOUR RESPITES FOR WEARY DOWNTOWN WORKERS DURING THE WEEK. CURBED IN 1826, IT BEGAN AS A MARSHY POOL IN THE SEVENTEENTH CENTURY, AND IS NOW USED FOR WADING AND SPECIAL EVENTS DURING THE SPRING AND SUMMER MONTHS.

The Frog Pond, Boston Common.

64. This boat landing and bridge are still employed by Bostonians today—winged Bostonians, that is. Swan boats grace the lake, and familiar contemporary sights such as the mounted statue of George Washington and the Arlington Street Church spire are visible in the background of this card. The Arlington Street Church was the first building in Boston's Back Bay, and was designed by Arthur Gilman. Its construction commenced in 1859. Harbridge House, the mansion at the right, stands near the spot now occupied by the Ritz Carlton Hotel.

Bridge and Boat Landing, Public Garden, Boston, Mass.

65. THIS VIEW INCLUDES A STATUE OF CHARLES SUMNER, THE MOST IMPORTANT BOSTONIAN THAT MOST PEOPLE TODAY (EVEN BOSTONIANS) KNOW NOTHING ABOUT. SUMNER WAS A HARVARD GRADUATE, AN AUTHOR, AND A WORLD TRAVELER. HE SERVED AS A U.S. SENATOR FROM 1852 UNTIL HIS DEATH IN 1874, AND WAS PERHAPS BEST KNOWN FOR HAVING BEEN CANED AT HIS DESK ON THE SENATE FLOOR TWO DAYS AFTER GIVING A VEHEMENT ANTI-SLAVERY SPEECH.

THE TREMONT STREET SUBWAY WAS AN IMPORTANT PART OF THE RAPID TRANSIT SYSTEM FROM ITS INCEPTION IN SEPTEMBER 1897. THIS CARD SHOWS WHAT WAS CALLED THE PUBLIC GARDEN INCLINE, WHICH WAS SEALED IN 1914 IN FAVOR OF THE BOYLSTON STREET PORTAL. WITH THE SUBWAY NOW COMPLETELY UNDERGROUND IN THIS AREA, THE STATUE HAS BEEN TURNED TO FACE THE STREET.

BOSTON, Mass.
Public Garden,
Entrance to
Subway.

U.S. 610.

66. ARTHUR SHURCLIFF WAS CONTRACTED TO DESIGN THE ZOO IN FRANKLIN PARK. AN APPRENTICE OF FREDERICK LAW OLMSTED, SHURCLIFF AUGMENTED THE PROUD DESIGN OF THE PARK OVER A PERIOD OF TWENTY YEARS, CREATING HABITAT FOR MANY ANIMALS, INCLUDING COUGAR, BEAR, ELK, AND, MOST IMPORTANT, ELEPHANTS. SEVERAL GENERATIONS ENJOYED THE PACHYDERMIC MEANDERING OF THREE VERY FAMOUS ELEPHANTS: WADDY, MOLLY, AND TONY. THE ZOO SURVIVED A PERIOD OF DECLINE DURING THE MIDDLE OF THE TWENTIETH CENTURY, BUT HAS WITNESSED A RESURRECTION OF SORTS RECENTLY. TODAY, HOWEVER, THERE ARE NO ELEPHANTS IN RESIDENCE.

965:—Elephant House and Walk, Franklin Park, Boston, Mass.

67. THE BOSTON COMMON'S PARKMAN BANDSTAND, UNDERUSED TODAY, WAS CREATED WITH FUNDS DONATED BY THE PARKMAN BEQUEST. IT IS AN EXAMPLE OF NEOCLASSICAL DESIGN.

NEARBY ON THE COMMON IS ANOTHER POPULAR STOP FOR TOURISTS: THE CENTRAL BURIAL GROUND, USED SINCE 1756. INTERRED IN THAT QUIET SPOT IS GILBERT STUART, THE ARTIST WHO PAINTED THE PORTRAIT OF GEORGE WASHINGTON NOW REPRODUCED ON THE ONE-DOLLAR BILL.

Band Stand in Common, Boston, Mass.

6138

68. ST. ALPHONSUS HALL, LOCATED ON MISSION HILL IN ROXBURY, IS PART OF THE MISSION CHURCH ON THE CORNER OF TREMONT AND ST. ALPHONSUS. THE HALL WAS ONCE A 1,100-SEAT THEATER CONNECTED TO A CONVENT AND SCHOOL. TODAY IT CONTINUES ITS FIGHT FOR SURVIVAL IN AN AREA OF RAPIDLY INCREASING PROPERTY VALUES, WHERE TOO MANY PROPERTY OWNERS HAVE LITTLE USE FOR BEAUTIFUL HISTORIC LANDMARKS THAT CANNOT BE TURNED INTO CHEAP HOUSING FOR STUDENTS FROM NEARBY COLLEGES.

St. Alphonsus Hall, Roxbury, Mass.

214773

69. Although it no longer stands, Chickering Hall was a major component of the music and cultural scene in Boston at the turn of the twentieth century. Constructed by Chickering & Sons, famous piano manufacturers, it graced Huntington Avenue near Massachusetts Avenue. In 1901, its second floor became the home of the Emerson College of Oratory, the college's first educational space.

CHICKERING HALL, BOSTON, MASS.

970

70. Although the signs advertise a "Matinee Today," modern-day visitors to Boston will have no such luck at the Castle Square Theatre. Located in Boston's South End, Castle Square is now a housing project, and the theater is gone. Famous actor Alfred Lunt began his career there with the Castle Square Theatre stock company.

17305

Castle Square Theatre,
Boston, Mass.

71. BOSTON'S MUSEUM OF FINE ARTS, FOUNDED AT THE BOSTON ATHENAEUM IN 1870, MOVED TO THIS FLAMBOYANT BUILDING IN COPLEY SQUARE IN 1876. THIS CARD DEPICTS THE MFA STANDING IN THE EXACT SPOT OF TODAY'S FAIRMONT COPLEY PLAZA HOTEL, NEAR TRINITY CHURCH. THE MFA MOVED TO ITS PRESENT LOCATION ON HUNTINGTON AVENUE IN 1909.

5558. THE ART MUSEUM, BOSTON, MASS.

72. THE LARGEST MUSEUM IN NEW ENGLAND, PLAYING HOST TO NEARLY ONE MILLION VISITORS ANNUALLY, THE MUSEUM OF FINE ARTS IS ACTUALLY IN ITS SECOND HOME HERE ON HUNTINGTON AVENUE. (THE ORIGINAL BUILDING WAS CONSTRUCTED ON COPLEY SQUARE IN 1875.) ARCHITECT GUY LOWELL WAS COMMISSIONED FOR THIS STRUCTURE, A MASSIVE 221,000-SQUARE-FOOT BUILDING THAT OPENED IN NOVEMBER 1909. SUBSEQUENT ADDITIONS TOTAL ANOTHER 403,000 SQUARE FEET. RENOWNED ARTIST JOHN SINGER SARGENT DECORATED THE ROTUNDA AND COLONNADE WITH PAINTINGS IN THE EARLY 1920S. SCULPTOR CYRUS EDWIN DALLIN CAST THE BEAUTIFUL STATUE OF AN INDIAN ON A HORSE, ENTITLED "THE APPEAL TO THE GREAT SPIRIT." THE MUSEUM HOUSES A TREASURE TROVE OF ART AND OBJECTS FROM AROUND THE GLOBE.

Entrance to Museum of Fine Arts,
Boston, Mass.

73. Like its nearby cousins—Symphony Hall, Chickering Hall, and Horticultural Hall—the Grand Opera House was a cultural colossus on Huntington Avenue, delighting thousands of spectators annually. An example of beaux-arts architecture, it stood in stark contrast to many of the Victorian designs that dotted the city landscape. During the 1960s, following a period of decline and after the defection of the opera company, the building was purchased by Northeastern University and razed during the expansion of the school's physical plant. The university's Speare Hall now graces the site.

87033   GRAND OPERA HOUSE, BOSTON, MASS.   *Copyright by Dadmun Co., Boston, 1909.*

74. THE OLD STATE HOUSE REPLACED THE WOODEN "OLD TOWN HOUSE" IN 1713. (NOTE THE TYPO—"TATE"—ON THE CARD.) IT WAS IN FRONT OF THIS BRICK BUILDING, THE SITE OF BOSTON'S EARLIEST MARKETPLACE, THAT BRITISH TROOPS, OR "LOBSTERBACKS," OPENED FIRE ON CITY DWELLERS WHO WERE HARASSING A BRITISH SENTRY IN MARCH 1770. PAUL REVERE'S ENGRAVING OF A HENRY PELHAM DRAWING OF THE SCENE IMMORTALIZED THE EVENT AS THE BOSTON MASSACRE.

THE OLD STATE HOUSE IS STILL ADORNED BY THE LION AND THE UNICORN. IRONICALLY, IT WAS FROM THE ORNAMENTAL BALCONY BENEATH THESE SYMBOLS OF THE BRITISH CROWN THAT THE CITIZENS OF BOSTON FIRST HEARD THE TEXT OF JEFFERSON'S DECLARATION OF INDEPENDENCE ON JULY 16, 1776.

OLD STATE HOUSE.

BOSTON, MASS.

75. THIS CARD DEPICTS THE REAR OF FANEUIL HALL ON THE QUINCY MARKET SIDE, LOOKING TOWARD WHAT IS NOW GOVERNMENT CENTER. THE HALL WAS A GIFT TO THE PEOPLE OF BOSTON FROM PETER FANEUIL IN 1742. REBUILT AFTER A FIRE IN 1762, AND ENLARGED BY CHARLES BULFINCH IN 1806, THIS SIMPLE BRICK BUILDING IS KNOWN AS THE "CRADLE OF LIBERTY" IN BOSTON. DEACON SHEM DROWNE'S COPPER GRASSHOPPER WEATHERVANE STANDS ATOP THE CUPOLA. VISITORS TO THE BUILDING TODAY ARE GREETED BY A STERN STATUE OF SAMUEL ADAMS, ONE OF BOSTON'S KEY LEADERS IN THE AMERICAN REVOLUTION AND COUSIN TO JOHN ADAMS, THE SECOND PRESIDENT OF THE UNITED STATES.

2886—*Farneil Hall, Boston, Mass.*

Souvenir Post Card Co., New York and Berlin.

76. Located in Boston's downtown financial district, at 20–42 Water Street, the National Shawmut Bank building still stands, although its namesake, Shawmut Bank, is defunct, having been purchased by Fleet Bank. Boston remains the financial power-house of New England.

A bit of trivia: The Fleet Center, home to the Celtics and Bruins, was originally to be called the Shawmut Center, and local sports reporters started referring to the building-to-be as the Mutt. Instead, it is now called the Vault.

THIS SPACE FOR WRITING

The National Shawmut Bank Building, Boston, Mass.

17445

77. Traffic, a staple in Boston—especially downtown—since the days of the horse and buggy, is evident in this turn-of-the-twentieth-century scene. Washington Street is jammed with shoppers bustling about the busy shopping district, just as it is today. Another Boston landmark, built in the Chicago style, is Filene's at 426 Washington. Designed by Daniel Burnham and Company in 1912, it has remained one of the most popular shopping stops in the city.

WASHINGTON STREET, AT SUMMER. BOSTON, MASS.

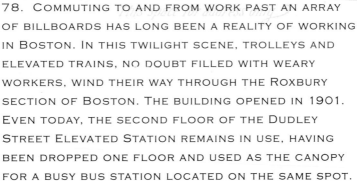

78. Commuting to and from work past an array of billboards has long been a reality of working in Boston. In this twilight scene, trolleys and elevated trains, no doubt filled with weary workers, wind their way through the Roxbury section of Boston. The building opened in 1901. Even today, the second floor of the Dudley Street Elevated Station remains in use, having been dropped one floor and used as the canopy for a busy bus station located on the same spot.

Roxbury, Mass. Dudley Street Elevated Station.

79. The Massachusetts Bay Transit Authority—MBTA for short—provides public transportation services throughout Boston and to outlying suburban areas via bus, subway, and trolley. At the turn of the last century, Boston's elevated rail system was a vital component that kept the masses moving. Here we see the Forest Hills terminal.

Forest Hills Elevated Station,
Boston, Mass.

80. THE GRANARY BURIAL GROUND'S EGYPTIAN-STYLE GRANITE GATEWAY MARKS THE ENTRANCE TO A "WHO'S WHO" OF BOSTON HISTORY. PAUL REVERE, SAM ADAMS, JOHN HANCOCK, PETER FANUEIL, ROBERT TREAT PAINE, BENJAMIN FRANKLIN'S PARENTS, AND THE VICTIMS OF THE BOSTON MASSACRE ARE ALL INTERRED HERE NEXT TO PARK STREET CHURCH. THE CEMETERY WAS NAMED FOR THE GRANARY THAT ONCE STOOD THERE (SEE CAPTION FOR CARD #3).

THIS SCENE, FROM 1904, DIFFERS ONLY SLIGHTLY FROM A CONTEMPORARY VIEW. THE PARK STREET T STATION (AT LOWER LEFT) IS VERY BUSY, WITH SHOPPERS AND WORKERS FILLING THE SIDEWALKS ON TREMONT STREET. THE PRESENT-DAY T STATION USES THE SAME ORANGE-TOPPED WHITE BUILDINGS AS THE SUBWAY DID THEN.

7573. GRANARY AND PARK STREET CHURCH, BOSTON, MASS.   COPYRIGHT, 1904, BY DETROIT PHOTOGRAPHIC CO.

Established 1660. Graves of J. Hancock,
Samuel Adams, Peter Faneuil, Paul Revere,
victims of Boston massacre, James Otis,
and Mother Goose.

POST CARD

QUALITY

MESSAGE MAY BE WRITTEN ON THIS SIDE.   ADDRESS ONLY ON THIS SIDE.

Place the Stamp here.
ONE CENT
for United States
and Island Possessions
Cuba, Canada and
Mexico.
TWO CENTS
for Foreign

81. THE ACADEMY AWARD–WINNING MOTION PICTURE *GLORY* MADE THE STORY OF THE 54TH REGIMENT OF MASSACHUSETTS FAMOUS IN 1989. HOWEVER, EVER SINCE ITS INSTALLATION IN 1897, THE ROBERT GOULD SHAW MEMORIAL, POSITIONED DIRECTLY ACROSS FROM THE STATE HOUSE STEPS AT THE TOP OF BEACON STREET, HAS REMINDED BOSTON CITIZENS OF THE HEROIC ACTS OF THE FIRST REGIMENT OF FREED AFRICAN-AMERICANS TO FIGHT FOR THE UNION IN THE CIVIL WAR. SHAW WAS ONLY TWENTY-SIX WHEN HE WAS KILLED LEADING HIS REGIMENT AGAINST FORT WAGNER, SOUTH CAROLINA, IN 1863. AUGUSTUS SAINT-GAUDENS WORKED ON THE SCULPTURE FOR THIRTEEN YEARS PRIOR TO ITS PLACEMENT.

The Show Memorial, Boston, Mass.

82. THE BUNKER HILL MONUMENT'S LESS FAMOUS COUSIN, THE DORCHESTER HEIGHTS MONUMENT, WAS FINISHED IN 1901 AND HOLDS A SPECIAL PLACE IN THE HEART OF HOMEGROWN BOSTONIANS. THIS PRETTY TOWER COMMEMORATES THE REVOLUTIONARY WAR VICTORY OF GENERAL GEORGE WASHINGTON AND HIS CONTINENTAL ARMY OVER THE BRITISH AT DORCHESTER HEIGHTS, WHICH CAUSED THE BRITISH TO "EVACUATE" THE CITY. BOSTON'S SCHOOLCHILDREN ARE ESPECIALLY THANKFUL FOR WASHINGTON'S VICTORY, AS THEY TRADITIONALLY RECEIVE AN EXTRA SCHOOL HOLIDAY EVERY YEAR COMMEMORATING THE DAY.

592. BOSTON, EVACUATION MONUMENT, DORCHESTER HEIGHTS.

P.131.

M.H.

83. THE SOLDIERS' AND SAILORS' MONUMENT ATOP FLAGSTAFF HILL IS JUST ONE FAMILIAR ASPECT OF BOSTON COMMON. THE HILL WAS ONCE USED FOR STASHING COLONIAL GUNPOWDER AND IS THE HIGHEST SPOT ON THE COMMON.

THE DOWNTOWN ANCHOR OF THE EMERALD NECKLACE, THE COMMON HAS BEEN A DISTINCT PARCEL SINCE 1634 AND HAS SERVED MANY USES. MILITIAS AND PROTESTERS HAVE MARCHED HERE— AND FOR THAT MATTER, SO HAVE COWS. IN 1823, CIVIL STATUTES WERE AMENDED TO ALLOW CITIZENS TO GRAZE ONLY ONE COW EACH. BOVINE VISITORS WERE BANNED ALTOGETHER IN 1830.

AN IRON FENCE HAS SURROUNDED THE COMMON SINCE 1735, BUT THE ORIGINAL WAS TAKEN DOWN FOR SCRAP METAL DURING WORLD WAR II. LEGEND HAS IT THAT THE FENCE WASN'T USED IN THE WAR EFFORT AFTER ALL, AND NOW LIES AT THE BOTTOM OF THE HARBOR.

THIS SPACE FOR WRITING

EOSTON, MASS. SOLDIERS' AND SAILORS' MONUMENT

For Correspondence.   For Address only.

84. THE MAGNIFICENT CHARLES BULFINCH—DESIGNED STATE HOUSE
ON BEACON HILL OCCUPIES LAND THAT WAS ONCE PART OF JOHN
HANCOCK'S ESTATE. IT WAS COMPLETED ON JANUARY 11, 1798.
EXTENSIONS WERE ADDED IN 1853 AND 1889. THE BUILDING STILL
HOUSES THE MASSACHUSETTS STATE GOVERNMENT, INCLUDING THE
GOVERNOR'S OFFICE AND THE LEGISLATURE.

NOTE THE AUTOMOBILE AT LOWER LEFT, THE PEOPLE ON THE
SIDEWALK, AND THE FLAGPOLES ATOP THE BUILDING. EARLY POST-
CARD PRINTERS WERE NOT ABOVE ADDING ITEMS OF INTEREST SUCH
AS THESE TO A CARD TO ENHANCE ITS SALABILITY. AUTOMOBILES,
AS WELL AS RANDOM FLAGPOLES, APPEAR FREQUENTLY IN OTHER
CARDS OF THE ERA, INCLUDING SOME IN THIS BOOK (NOTE THE
REMARKABLY SIMILAR CAR IMAGE IN CARD #48).

905 State House. Boston, Mass.

85. CHARLES BULFINCH DESIGNED MANY OF BOSTON'S MOST BEAUTIFUL AND MEMORABLE BUILDINGS, BUT THE MASSACHUSETTS STATE HOUSE MIGHT BE THE MOST FAMOUS OF ALL HIS PROGENY. NOW MUCH LARGER THAN SHOWN HERE, THE STATE HOUSE HAS JUST UNDERGONE A CONTEMPORARY RENOVATION. THE GILDED COPPER DOME WAS INSTALLED BY PAUL REVERE AND SONS IN 1802. IT WAS TEMPORARILY BLACKED OUT DURING WORLD WAR II SO IT COULD NOT BE USED AS A LANDMARK IN THE EVENT OF AN ENEMY AIR RAID, BUT REMAINS A BRILLIANT LANDMARK ON BEACON HILL. A STATUE OF CIVIL WAR HERO GENERAL JOSEPH HOOKER, A NATIVE OF HADLEY, MASSACHUSETTS, STANDS PERPETUAL WATCH.

514. BOSTON, STATE HOUSE AND HOOKER STATUE.

Dear Nellie

Juli.

S. Boston, 9, 15, 05

Your postal received with many thanks. Would
have written sooner, but had no time. Remember me to everybody

86. Recently named by the *Boston Phoenix* as Boston's "best unnoticed public fountain," the Brewer Fountain depicts mythical figures. Gardner Brewer originally had this huge fountain installed on his lawn on Beacon Street, having brought the work back from the 1867 Paris Exhibition. It is a replica of a fountain commissioned by Napoleon III in 1855. Brewer donated the fountain to the city in the 1870s.

This nighttime winter scene is reminiscent of Boston's popular annual First Night Celebration held every December 31 downtown and on the Common.

BOSTON, BREWER FOUNTAIN AND STATE HOUSE AT NIGHT.

87. BESIDE THE PARK STREET CHURCH CAN BE FOUND THE FINAL RESTING PLACE OF MANY OF BOSTON'S MOST FAMOUS PATRIOTIC CITIZENS. THE GRANARY BURIAL GROUND IS HOME TO THIS HANDSOME STONE MARKING THE GRAVE OF JOHN HANCOCK. HANCOCK'S GRAVE MARKER, LIKE HIS TRADEMARK SIGNATURE ON THE DECLARATION OF INDEPENDENCE, IS EASILY SEEN FROM AFAR.

Boston, Mass. Grave of John Hancock.

88. THE FIRST OWNER OF THIS HOUSE WAS A WEALTHY MERCHANT NAMED ROBERT HOWARD, BUT TO BOSTONIANS THIS MODEST DWELLING AT 19 NORTH SQUARE WILL ALWAYS BE PAUL REVERE'S HOUSE. THE FAMOUS MIDNIGHT RIDER PURCHASED THE HOUSE IN 1770 AND LEFT FROM HERE TO WARN THE COUNTRYSIDE OF THE IMPENDING ARRIVAL OF THE REDCOATS IN APRIL 1775.

WHEN PAUL REVERE OWNED THE HOUSE, IT PROBABLY LOOKED SIMILAR TO THIS. TODAY'S VISITORS SEE A STRUCTURE THAT MORE CLOSELY RESEMBLES THE LOOK OF THE HOUSE DURING HOWARD'S TIME (CA. 1680), BEFORE THE THIRD FLOOR WAS EXTENDED. THE BUILDING HAS GONE THROUGH SEVERAL INCARNATIONS, SERVING AS A CANDY STORE, CIGAR FACTORY, BANK, AND VEGETABLE MARKET. IT WAS LOVINGLY RESTORED AND HAS BEEN CAREFULLY MAINTAINED SINCE 1902. THE PAUL REVERE MEMORIAL ASSOCIATION HAS RUN THE BUILDING AS A MUSEUM SINCE 1908.

Home of Paul Revere, Boston, Mass.

89. HENRY HOBSON RICHARDSON, ARCHITECT OF THE NEARBY TRINITY CHURCH, ALSO DESIGNED THIS PRETTY CHURCH AND ITS SQUARE TOWER, TOPPED BY A DECORATIVE FRIEZE AND ARCHES. THE FRIEZE IS INTERESTING BECAUSE FRÉDÉRIC AUGUSTE BARTHOLDI, THE SCULPTOR OF THE STATUE OF LIBERTY, MODELED IT. IT IS ALSO NOTABLE BECAUSE IT IS SAID TO DISPLAY THE IMAGES OF MANY FAMOUS MASSACHUSETTS CITIZENS: EMERSON, HAWTHORNE, LONGFELLOW, AND SUMNER. TRUMPETING ANGELS DISPLAYED ON THE 176-FOOT BELL TOWER HAVE GIVEN THE CHURCH THE NICKNAME OF "CHURCH OF THE HOLY BEAN BLOWERS."

First Baptist Church.

Boston, Mass.

My Sunday Home

No. 5013

Published by The New England News Company Boston Mass., Leipzig and Dresden.

90. This is an interesting view of Copley Square. Notice the Hotel Westminster, shown at center. Not quite a hotel in the modern sense, it was actually more akin to today's upscale apartments and condominiums.

Ironically, considering its would-be downtown neighbors today, the building was too tall originally. The city ordered the two uppermost stories removed because the building exceeded the 80-foot maximum allowed by zoning.

In the late 1960s, the building was demolished to make way for the new John Hancock Tower.

Copley Square, Boston, Mass.

17299

91. FOUNDED IN 1848 BY AN ACT OF THE GREAT AND GENERAL COURT OF MASSACHUSETTS, THE BOSTON PUBLIC LIBRARY WAS THE NATION'S FIRST LARGE CITY LIBRARY, AND THE FIRST MAJOR LIBRARY TO BE TAX-FUNDED. ITS FIRST HOME WAS MASON STREET, BUT AFTER FOUR YEARS THE INSTITUTION MOVED TO BOYLSTON STREET, IN 1858. THAT BUILDING ALSO PROVED TOO SMALL, AND IN 1895 THE LIBRARY MOVED TO ITS PRESENT COPLEY SQUARE LOCATION UPON COMPLETION OF THE CLASSICALLY INSPIRED MCKIM, MEAD, AND WHITE—DESIGNED COLOSSUS SHOWN HERE.

Boston, Mass., Delivery Room. Public Library.

92. WITH THE POSSIBLE EXCEPTION OF THE OLD NORTH CHURCH, TRINITY CHURCH IS THE BEST KNOWN OF BOSTON'S HOUSES OF WORSHIP. DESIGNED BY HENRY HOBSON RICHARDSON, IT WAS BUILT BETWEEN 1872 AND 1877 AND COST "ONLY" $750,000 TO BUILD. THE MASSIVE TOWER IS SUPPORTED BY TWO THOUSAND WOOD PILES ARRANGED IN A NINETY-FOOT SQUARE. NOW A NATIONAL HISTORIC LANDMARK, TRINITY CHURCH STANDS NEXT TO ONE OF THE MOST RECOGNIZABLE SIGHTS ON THE MODERN BOSTON SKYLINE, THE GLASS-WALLED JOHN HANCOCK TOWER.

502. BOSTON, TRINITY CHURCH.

93. Surrounded today by much taller modern buildings, St. Paul's Episcopal Church is Boston's first real example of Greek Revival style. Built between 1819 and 1820 by the eventual architect of Quincy Market, Alexander Parris, the building employs a temple façade. St. Paul's faces the "Brimstone Corner" of Boston Common—so dubbed because of the fiery rhetoric of many of the Congregational pastors who preached in the nearby Park Street Church.

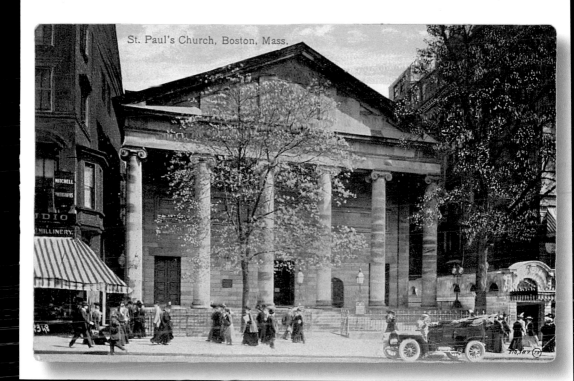

St. Paul's Church, Boston, Mass.

94. Joshua Humphrey, who designed the U.S.S. *Constitution* in 1797, surely could not have imagined the success his vessel would achieve. Undefeated in forty-two battles during the War of 1812, Old Ironsides was so named because its massive oak planking was seemingly impenetrable. Paul Revere and Sons supplied the copper sheathing that protected the lower hull from wood-boring worms. She served as a navy training vessel into the 1900s, and is shown here with the extra deck that was then used as a barracks.

The *Constitution* probably owes its preservation to an Oliver Wendell Holmes poem that immortalized the vessel and heightened public awareness of its place in American history. Today, the much-beloved ship remains one of the top tourist destinations in the city.

Old (Ironsides) Constitution, Boston, Mass.

2616

95. THIS MARVELOUS STRUCTURE ON CLARENDON STREET WAS THE FIRST MAJOR BUILDING IN BOSTON CONSTRUCTED BY THE JOHN HANCOCK LIFE INSURANCE COMPANY. THE COMPANY LATER (1949) TRANSFERRED ITS FLAG TO A SKYSCRAPER ON BERKELEY STREET, AND THEN, IN 1976, MOVED INTO TODAY'S GLEAMING, GLASS-WALLED JOHN HANCOCK TOWER, DESIGNED BY I. M. PEI.

John Hancock Life Insurance Co. Building, Boston, Mass.

96. DESIGNED TO BRING ITS PATIENTS OUT INTO THE COOLING, FRESH AIR OF THE OCEAN, THIS HOSPITAL SHIP BEGAN A TRADITION OF CARING CONTINUED TODAY AT THE TUFTS—NEW ENGLAND MEDICAL CENTER FLOATING HOSPITAL FOR CHILDREN. THE SHIP PICTURED FIRST CAME TO USE AS A FLOATING HOSPITAL IN 1894, AND, ACCORDING TO THE MEDICAL CENTER'S WEB SITE, SAILED BOSTON HARBOR "ENCOURAGING MOTHERS TO PARTICIPATE IN THEIR CHILDREN'S HEALTH CARE." THE REVEREND RUFUS TOBEY RAISED MONEY TO PURCHASE THE SHIP AFTER WITNESSING BOSTON MOTHERS FIGHT A LOSING BATTLE AGAINST SUMMERTIME HEAT. THE SHIP WAS DESTROYED BY FIRE IN 1927.

Hospital Ship, Boston, Mass.

97. CRUISE SHIPS REMAIN A STAPLE IN THE LIFE OF BOSTON HARBOR. IN THIS EARLY TWENTIETH-CENTURY SCENE FROM THE COMMONWEALTH PIER, BYSTANDERS WAVE GOOD-BYE TO DEPARTING RELATIVES AND FRIENDS. TODAY, COMMONWEALTH PIER IS THE SITE OF THE BOSTON WORLD TRADE CENTER. THE HEADHOUSE PORTION OF THE ORIGINAL PIER WAS CAREFULLY PRESERVED WHEN THE TRADE CENTER WAS CONSTRUCTED.

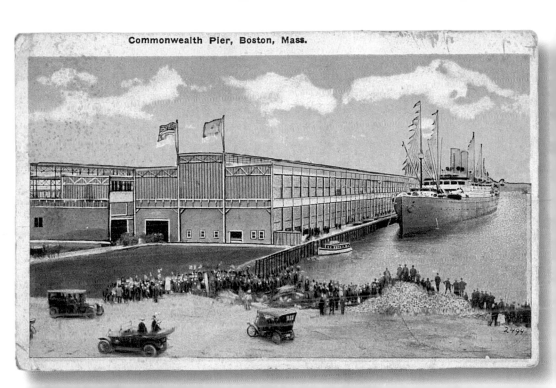

Commonwealth Pier, Boston, Mass.

2494

98. FERRY SERVICE IS IMPORTANT TO ANY CITY BORDERED BY WATER, AND EVEN TODAY SOME BOSTONIANS RELY ON FERRIES TO TRAVEL TO AND FROM THE CITY ON BUSINESS OR FOR PLEASURE. HERE, A BOAT CROSSES THE HARBOR TOWARD THE EAST BOSTON WATERFRONT. TUNNELS AND THE TROLLEY LINE UNDER THE HARBOR THROUGH THE EAST BOSTON TUNNEL HELPED RUN MANY OF THE FERRIES OUT OF BUSINESS.

Boston Harbor showing E. Boston Water Front and Ferry.

99. Looming just above 635 feet, Great Blue Hill, in Milton, was used as a vantage point during the Revolution. Lawrence Rotch, son of a prominent Boston family, built the first weather station at the summit. Fireworks heralded its opening on January 31, 1885. Today, the Blue Hill Meteorological Observatory is the oldest continuously operated weather observatory in the United States. In fact, a mercury barometer installed there in 1887 remains in daily use. The highest wind gust ever recorded at the observatory—186 miles per hour—came on September 21, 1938, during the Great New England Hurricane. The coldest temperature, −21°F, was recorded on February 9, 1934.

The stone tower pictured on the postcard was replaced with a taller concrete structure in 1908.

BLUE HILL OBSERVATORY. BLUE HILLS, MASS.

Did you ever climb Blue Hill?

3-12-07

100. BEANS OF EVERY TYPE, SLOW-BAKED IN MOLASSES (PREFERABLY IN A BRICK OVEN) WITH SALT PORK, HAVE LONG BEEN A FAVORITE DISH IN BOSTON AND A SATURDAY-NIGHT STAPLE SINCE COLONIAL DAYS. ALONG WITH BEING KNOWN AS THE HUB, BOSTON SOON ATTRACTED THE MONIKER OF BEANTOWN, THANKS TO THIS TASTY NEW ENGLAND DELICACY.

MOST OF THE MOLASSES THAT BOSTON MANUFACTURERS IMPORTED FROM THE WEST INDIES WAS TURNED INTO RUM. THE PURITY DISTILLING COMPANY'S RIVETED STEEL TANK ON COMMERCIAL STREET, CONTAINING APPROXIMATELY 2.3 MILLION GALLONS OF MOLASSES, RUPTURED SHORTLY AFTER NOON ON JANUARY 15, 1919, SENDING A BROWN WAVE SOME THIRTY-FIVE FEET HIGH THROUGH THE STREETS. THE GREAT MOLASSES FLOOD RESULTED IN 21 PEOPLE KILLED AND NEARLY 150 INJURED.

YOU DONT KNOW

BEANS

UNTIL YOU COME TO

BOSTON

COPYRIGHTED 1911 A. PANOSIAN

To learn more

🔖 THE BOSTONIAN SOCIETY
OLD STATE HOUSE
206 WASHINGTON STREET
BOSTON, MASSACHUSETTS 02109-1713
(617) 720-1713

🔖 THE MASSACHUSETTS
HISTORICAL SOCIETY
1154 BOYLSTON STREET
BOSTON, MA 02215-3695
(617) 536-1608

🔖 SOCIETY FOR THE PRESERVATION
OF NEW ENGLAND ANTIQUITIES
141 CAMBRIDGE STREET
BOSTON, MA 02114
(617) 227-3956

Helpful references

Bacon, Edward. *Boston: A Guidebook*. Boston: Ginn and Company, 1903.

Bergen, Phillip. *Old Boston in Early Photographs, 1850–1918*. New York: Dover, 1990.

Corbett, William. *Literary New England: A History and Guide*. Boston: Faber and Faber, 1993.

Drake, Samuel Adams. *Old Landmarks and Historic Personages of Boston*. Detroit: Singing Tree Press, 1970.

Fagundes, David, and Grant, Anthony. *The Mini Rough Guide to Boston*. London: Rough Guides, 2000.

Honig, Donald. *The Boston Red Sox: An Illustrated History*. New York: Prentice Hall, 1990.

McClellan, William B. *Pocket Guide for the Stranger in Boston*. Self-published, 1876.

McNulty, Elizabeth. *Boston Then and Now*. San Diego: Thunder Bay, 1999.

Moore, Scott. *100 Years of the Tremont Street*

Subway. Article on the New England Transportation website: members.aol.com/netransit/private/tss/tss.html

O'Connor, Thomas. *Building a New Boston*. Boston: Northeastern Univ., 1993.

O'Connor, Thomas. *Civil War Boston: Home Front & Battlefield*. Boston: Northeastern Univ., 1997.

O'Connor, Thomas. *The Hub*. Boston: Northeastern Univ., 2001.

O'Connor, Thomas. *South Boston: My Home Town*. Boston: Northeastern Univ., 1988.

Sanmarco, Anthony Mitchell. *Boston: A Century of Progress*. Dover: Arcadia, 1995.

Southworth, Susan, and Michael Southworth. *AIA Guide to Boston*. Guilford, Ct.: Globe Pequot, 1992.

Ulrich, Laurel. *A Beginner's Boston*. Cambridge: Ward, 1970.

Wilson, Susan. *Boston Sites and Insights*. Boston: Beacon, 1994.

Helpful websites

www.lenoxhotel.com

www.fairmont.com

www.bambinomusical.com

www.bostonparkplaza.com

www.boston.com

www.bostonherald.com

www.simmons.edu

www.sallys-place.com

www.bostonphoenix.com

www.paulrevere.org

www.mbta.com

www.boston-online.com

www.trolleystop.com

www.massport.com

www.bostonfamilyhistory.com

www.wai.com

www.fablevision.com

www.lifespan.org

www.bu.edu

www.bostonhistory.org

www.bostonseaport.com

www.lighthouse.cc

About the Author

EARL BRECHLIN is a Registered Maine Guide and author of several books, including *An Adventure Guide to Maine*, *Hiking on Mt. Desert Island*, and *Paddling the Waters of Mt. Desert Island*. He is editor of the *Mount Desert Islander* and former editor of the *Bar Harbor Times*. An adjunct faculty member at College of the Atlantic in Bar Harbor, he was named Maine Journalist of the Year in 1997 and has served as president of the Maine Press Association and the New England Press Association.

Acknowledgments First and foremost, the largest share of credit for this book goes to John Bishop, who prowled the halls of Boston's libraries and reading rooms for hours doing research. Special thanks also to Link McKie, journalism professor at Northeastern University, for linking me up with John.

The cards in this book come from a variety of sources, including the author's collection and the collections of Carl Brechlin, of Meriden, Connecticut, and Barbara Saunders, of Rockland, Maine. No amount of thanks can properly credit all the love and support and inspiration I've received from my wife, Roxie.

Of course, special thanks to Karin Womer, Terry Brégy, and all the folks at Down East Books. ☙ E. B. ❧

I would like to thank Earl Brechlin for his patience and advice; Angela Dombrowski, Jane Holtz Kay, and Clay McShane for their help in my research; Jack Grinold, Northeastern University's sports information impresario and Boston history guru; and Link McKie and Northeastern's School of Journalism for the opportunity to work on this project. Thanks also go to the Northeastern University Athletic Department, the Boston College Library, the Boston University History Department, and the Paul Revere House. Last but not least, I am grateful to my fiancée, Andrea Petrucci, and to my family and friends for their love and support.
☙ J. B. ❧